CW00474062

We Saw It All

Julian Bisl.

First published 13th of January 2023
Published in the UK by
Fly on the Wall Press
56 High Lea Rd
New Mills
Derbyshire
SK22 3DP

www.flyonthewallpress.co.uk
ISBN:9781913211912

A CIP Catalogue record for this book is available from the
British Library.

Printed in Great Britain by Severn, Gloucester

Preface

These poems were written over seven or so years at a time when daily headlines brought more evidence of climate change and our increasing disconnection with nature. I'm a journalist and, for a time, worked as an environment reporter, hoping perhaps that my reports might go some small way to change hearts and minds. I think it's fair to say I failed which might explain some of the frustration and sadness expressed in many of the poems. I also feel that, with collective will, change does happen, as with the Back From the Brink initiative to rescue the Little Whirlpool Ramshorn Snail you'll read about.

That said, quite a few poems are downbeat, even downright gloomy. I hope that doesn't translate to despair because that way lies inaction and, as poems like *Guerrilla* make clear, there's plenty that can be done, for example not viewing animals and habitat as infinite resources to be exploited. Nature can and will fight back back, if given the chance.

That also may explain the lack of lyric poetry here, which necessarily centres around the "I". I've tried to harness my journalistic background to offer a form of poetic reportage rather than personal hand-wringing.

I hope you also find a dash of humour and forgive the occasional soapbox moment in the more political poems. *No caveats, we need to see change.*

Contents

A Taster

Mains

Afters

"the task he undertakes is numbering sands and drinking oceans dry."

William Shakespeare
Richard II

A TASTER

For Starters

It was the Californian ocean that served them up:
mussels already cooked, not in white wine and garlic
            but basted in saline

roasted in coves, poached in the brine of Bodega Bay—
scores of dead molluscs washed up on rocks
            seared asleep in their beds

record-breaking heat turning the sea into consommé,
a lethal broth simmering the sweet orange meats
            clamped behind the doors

of individual mini-ovens, leaving marine biologists
baffled: were the ready meals a one-off special
            or a taste of things to come?

Lobster

Pepsi—it was the brand he grew up
with—the sweet memory of it, the
familiar tang of aluminium. Each night
cradled in a cot of cans, suckled on
bottles, sleeping on a seabed littered
with plastic toys, tops spinning on
the floor. Every one of them Pepsi.
He dressed up in armour, it became
a habit (with a Pepsi logo), hung out
with a pile of drifters, washed up
types who didn't even look fine on the
surface. They all drank Pepsi. He got
a tattoo, festooned in red and blue,
he soon became a brand ambassador,
the extravagant fandangle spangled
on a hand. But he threw it all away.
Bottled it. Abandoned, he washed up
on a beach, that's where I found him.
Junked, with only a Pepsi filigree.
Even his mother sent him packing.

Poached Salmon

            Sluggish and sun-struck she flounders
        in parboiled water, unable to spawn,
inadequate cladding stripped away

            by suffocating heat. The fast current
        is electrified, charged by the weather,
a new element in her early demise.

            She's struggled against the obstinate
        Columbia River to give birth upstream,
driven by the season's turn. For so long

            suspended in a star-calmed ocean,
        she held her own against a crimson sun.
Now her rainbows dull to drizzling pain.

            The river is a crypt lit by a dripping
        sky. Hot wax scalds her back, pink flesh
pales beneath the iron scales. Her roe blacken

            to full-stops inside. When clouds come
        they hurl rain that kettles the water.
There's no let-up from the nettle bed

            in the Columbia. The top floor is filling
        with smoke, in the distance a siren sounds
as the climate starts to sharpen its knife.

The Pirates Scuttled The Ship

We had fire in the porthole when we stormed the Ark,
        overwhelmed the gunwales,
        clambered over bulwarks,
zipped up the ladders, briskets against fur
        to the slabber and shiver
        of hooves on timber,
fo'c'sle to bowsprit was creatures displaced
so we keelhauled a handful to give us more space.

Oh they squabbled and nickered as they trotted down the plank
        and we knocked back the Black Jack
        as the pintaroos sank
Kerrang went a pangolin off the aft-most mast
        full fathom five
        went the funnel-eared bats
but the sharks they were slathering for even more bait
so we keelhauled a handful to give us more space.

Then the sea became a soup, a foaming of paws,
        they twizzled in the jetsam
        as we burst into applause
and the great auk sank to a *yo-ho-ho*
        while the surf took a quagga,
        a moa and a dodo.
But a pirate needs quarter for his pieces of eight
so we keelhauled a handful to give us more space.

We headed for landfall where we plundered and pillaged,
        we cutlassed the cycads
        and hornswaggled villages

we scuttled the rivers with small plastic beads
then scuppered the buttercups,
        and even the bees
until nothing was left for a pirate to chase,
we'd keelhauled the lot to give us more space.

Pangolin

a splendor
which man in all his vileness cannot
set aside—
         Marianne Moore, The Pangolin, 1936

Part botanical, part mechanical dragon
         Marianne considered you more
Artichoke than mammal, more plant
         than anteater, your pine-cone whorls
Nestled snug among the jungle under-scrub.
         Ardently pursued for your aluminium
Glossiness, armoured dinosaur, your snakeskin
         plates were scraped quite clean by
Opportunistic traffickers; exotic crocs served up
         as mysterious elixirs to quicken
Lactation or help drain pus. Alas, uncanny pangolin,
         maybe your foil-covered flesh
Incubated more than a quick fix, your silver plates
         Stripped by unscrupulous poachers,
Name made notorious by those who sickled open
         the last cans of your slatted metal backs.

Remember When Hippos Used to Swim?

Thirty dirty hippos
trudge towards the welcome
slosh of Lake Ngami,
once five-star spa for stressed
creatures, now one-star dive
decimated by drought.

Their hot bulks baked all day
beneath a punishing
Botswana sun. Decked from
grubby snout to hard hoof
in leather, the hulking
hipps should be weather proofed:

hides warding off the worst
but all-day lumbering
through thin depleted scrub
makes the herd desperate
to lie down and wallow
in a long cool mud bath.

They plunge in fully clothed
but the thick mire grips them,
holds them close. The hippos
panic, flounder deeper
into the gluey folds
of ravenous black sludge.

Hungry vultures circle,
sizing up the mud-braised
hippopotamuses.
Packed tight, they sizzle like
sausages in a huge
African frying pan.

Useful Creatures

(A Golden Shovel from *My Friend Tree, Lorine Niedecker*)

Nature as always seen through the lens of the I,
hooked on utility for mankind. See how the rose
plucked and unpetalled, metamorphoses from

flower to oil, same process that subjugates a marsh,
turns a worm's blood to black in the squealing mud.
Every plant presents as advantage—kelps and algae

curatives for ailing hearts, extracts of equisetum
effective to stem bleeding. Cricket bats from willows,
crucified moths accessorise Darwin's box. Sweet

slime sold as detox, the bankable language of green
translates hedges into cash. And what of the noisy
wild-winged mosquitoes, prinking at night like birds,

immaterial as that other species with its arms and
armaments, useless even as foodstuff for frogs?

Highlights of Mining for Gold in Indonesia

Look inside the lovely ring, at a gold chain, your piercing,
they become a mirror when buffed. Beneath the lustre,
watch as men with chainsaws appear from a clearing.

Your eyes settle on an orangutan, a Tapanuli grooming
her golden fur in the sun. She's one of eight hundred
living inside that lovely ring, a gold chain, your piercing.

Under the smoky canopy, she spends her days feasting
on mangosteen, golden-fleshed durian, rattan liana
until the two men with chainsaws set to work clearing.

Tapanuli freezes, conscious her infrequent offspring
are popular as pets in Taiwan. She eyes the predators
who live inside lovely rings, a gold chain, your piercing.

She's quiet thunder and lumber, a gold vein threading
together diminishing jungle but an inconvenient gorilla
to the two men with chainsaws. They work on, clearing

until all the mangosteen, durian and liana are nothing
but stumps, part of *an ambitious sustainability agenda*.
Look inside the long gold chain, listen to the piercing
chainsaw, see how smoke rises above the clearing.

Sulawesi Warty Pigs

Only the barest trace of us remains.

No more than a flicker, campfires quickened the walls until,
      by stroke and erosion of bone, you made us.

You hammered us into stone for millennia,
      daubed in blood and ochre:

short-legged, coarse-haired grunters,
days spent graunching roots, fallen fruit.

      Maybe you saw an opportunity - after all, *those squalid
      animals* were plentiful?

Your method of capturing us was so crude,
      hard to believe
all you had were flints and knives.

All you had were flints and knives.
      Hard to believe
your method of capturing us was so crude.

      Animals were plentiful,
      maybe you saw an opportunity after all those squalid

days spent graunching roots, fallen fruit?
Short-legged coarse-haired grunters,
you hammered us into stone for millennia,
      daubed in blood and ochre.

By stroke and erosion of bone you made us
no more than a flicker. Campfires quickened the walls until

only the barest trace of us remained.

The Last Days of the Giraffe

She stared down from her beige tower block
onto an alien plain: zig-zag of roofs, wingless
cranes, zebra crossings and a sea of litter,
the new neighbours behaved like bushpigs.

Once she used to hoof it down the Thames
reflecting on The Shard, to graze on acacias
next to London Bridge. Her rubber-lined lips
twitched at the soft waft of lemony wattle

like a sengi scenting ticks. After she fell
from the tallest of stories, they tried
to reassemble her into an okapi, giraffe
in almost all but neck. But the waiting list

was way too long for a specialist in backs.
Towards the end of her lengthy decline,
a chain of restaurants was named after her
but *chicken pide* wasn't exactly her thing.

She stayed a towering presence in the memory
of residents who laughed about her high-minded
taste for mimosa, how they nicknamed her *BT*,
how it was all a big game and then it wasn't.

Bushmeat

First up are bushbucks,
        dappled pelts like Bambi,
                slapped onto blood-spattered slabs
                    at the open-air abattoir,
carcasses garroted, tendered to a fire
                    to burn off fur.

The stench of blistered flesh
        drifts across corrugated shacks,
                a butcher scrubs blackened rashers
                    clean of ash.
This meat is so good people will smell your soup
                from the UK.

Charred and butchered,
        prime cuts are smoked,
                sparks strobe the furred air.
                    Bluebottles wallow in sticky runnels
made murkier by soot, the concrete floor bloody
                    with run-off.

A woman puts up a stall, a crock
        of iced blood to keep off flies.
                As she shuts, she washes her hands
                    in the malodorous bowl.
Her customers will cram the mouths of suitcases,
                catch flights home.

Snow Leopard

protection (n) preservation from injury or harm; the activity of
protecting someone or something

The empty cage tells its own tale   Beauty and the Beast
reworked

       a fairy-tale creature   beneath the brutish exterior

not killed   *euthanised*   *murdered* they scream on Twitter
       @beccassaurus: *[they are not ours]*
       @DudleyZoo: *[a keeper error]*

close-up pictures   the shots   reveal firepit eyes
       luminous monochrome coat
             paws   dinner-plate size

I throw my heart into the outrage
       like: *[why no tranquilliser lads?]*
       like: *[zookeeper failed at his job]*
       like: *[Justice for Margaash]*

       a threatened animal pads through a closed zoo
but is no threat
       the animal they were protecting
       goes unprotected

       a threatened animal from gold-filled mountains
is no threat
       the animal is protected
       to protect profits

to protect the world from a threatened cat
       the marksman only took one shot

to protect the threatened cat from the world
        we only had one shot

            our empty cages tweet their own tale

            #hashtag: *epicfail*

To The Man Who Poisoned 420 Eagles In A Year

Did you watch by Snowy River as your bomb went off
while she glided on an updraft of warm summer air?

Did you smile as her lights dulled and engine stalled
five thousand feet above the ground?

Did you blink as her nine-foot wingspan swerved into a loop,
lurched into a sudden double-dip?

Did you beam as her landing gear seized up
as she hurtled towards earth?

Did you laugh as her portholes shuttered black, grin
as her tail fin skimmed a stand of plum-coloured pines?

Did you cheer as her fuselage smashed on the mountainside,
as she writhed beneath a plume of brown smoke?

Did you joke to yourself as you raked through her debris
praying for signs of no life?

Did you strop a knife before you spliced her windpipe
to cut short her last hoarse squawk?

Did you warm your hands on her breast as you stuffed
her feathered wreckage into a burlap sack?

Did you stand back as the head was severed and skidded
into sharp claws of gorse?

Did your heart burst with pride as you piled the skulls
knee-high in your tumbledown barn?

Did you tell the court you felt no remorse while planes on fire
fell like rain from a cloudless Australian sky?

Dung Beetles

Strange that catastrophe should announce itself
        on such small feet
among such humble collectors of dirt,
        street-cleaners, shovellers of stools,
        tunnellers through filth.

Ancient Egyptians saw gods in them, suns in dung
        shaped into spheres
dragged into creepy-crawly underworlds.
        Guided by starry skies, they deep-cleaned fields,
        deodorised cattle dumps.

Photographers fawned over tigers, meercats,
        svelte giraffes
while caddis flies withered in the wings.
        No lightbulbs exploded as spiders dived for cover
        beneath piles of calcified scat.

Globetrotting beetles wade through cesspits
        teeming with tailings,
cowpats contaminated by worm controls.
        Bugs that make the world go round push up
        the daisies, while the planet goes to shit.

At A Ceremony To Mark
A Million Ways To Drive
Small Creatures To Extinction.

No. 999,999: The Tansy Beetle

Ladies and Gentlemen, this last but one
entry demonstrates man's ingenuity in
this crowded field, home to the last scraps
of emerald tinsel known as the tansy beetle,
tiny lacquer-backed bugs whose foiled torsos
were excorticated to decorate elaborate
Victorian cocktail hats,

                            tens of thousands
of wingcases pinned by milliners to creations
fabricated from rabbit-fur, as if the insect
world were a creepy crawly haberdashery
to embellish ostrich-feathered hats. Such
painstaking attention to extinction in pursuit
of sequins makes this entry worthy of nothing
but the highest distinction.

Darwin's Beetle Box

'Whenever I hear of the capture of rare beetles,
I feel like an old war-horse at the sound of a trumpet'
— Charles Darwin

Sequins arranged in linear sequence
on liver-spotted cloth, each pinned
vertically through the mesothorax,
handwritten Latin names engraved
in faded ink on paper gravestones.

*

Whether a library of diversity or innate
greed for completeness, collectors saw
scarabs and longhorns as loose change.
Now they're dwindling savings, ill-gotten
gains from a grassy bank we all robbed.

*

Hard to square with Darwin's brilliance:
this box of beetle corpses, filaments
dimmed by a dollop of ethyl acetate
dropped into the great man's killing jar
until their miniature clockwork stopped.

To All The Insects I Ever Squished

I apologise. For my addiction to squish, for its satisfying
half-rhyme with *delicious*, for its down-to-earth equivalence

with *murder*. I apologise for those wing-beats stilled
between twisted finger and thumb, for the thrilling thrum

of upended surrender. I apologise to you spiders, for sluicing
you from my basins, for watching you shrivel into raisins.

I apologise for the tingling strings of the ultraviolet zapper,
for the dazzle and crackle as your tiny fingers shook

as you grasped at the blue bars. I apologise for the jars
loaded with watered-down raspberry jam to ambush you

as you darted towards my back door. To all you aphids
raving on a rosebud, I apologise for the tasteless relish

of puréeing you by hand into lemon and lime jam. To all you
trampled ants, all you cursive gnats and copperplate moths

singed by my citronella flames, I apologise. For the opiate
of spilling a bug's sweet blood, for cans of Vapona and Raid,

for the sticky yellow papers suspended from a curtain rail
where you flailed like tortured saints. To you wasps, despite

your gratuitous attacks, despite your sun-splashed shimmies
over picnics in your flaxens and blacks, I apologise for prizing

a sandwich more than your lives. To you blood-drunk mosquitoes,
spinning the dark with your bobbins and pins, no redress

but a scintilla of regret, for it was self-defence, the fist quicker
than live and let live. To all you hoverers, botherers, to all of you

multifaceted variations on flies, I apologise. Know you were never
to blame, it was simply the congenital human urge to eliminate.

Insectageddon

How we long for the waft of naphthalene   mothballs
     reek of crushed neem
     swirl of citronella candle smoke
       wormwood   rues you used   to get rid of us

even the escalation was quaint
     helter-skelter of sticky papers   swatters   zappers
     random muggings in ultraviolet bars
       blasts of *Vapona*   *Raid*   hiss of *Wondercide*

until your fixation was lifted
to a shriller pitch   swept across countless acres
     weaponised tractors   deployed indiscriminate fire
one swipe at blight   took out hoverflies   bees

larkspur   campion   scabiouses   wilted with the aphids
     into a reinforced maize   you sprayed
     merciless rain   in clouds
       over bugs   huddled for shelter

our weakened casings   let toxins in
     dripping   into pools of meaty soups
     devoured by ravenous dragonflies
       grassy pressés   sipped by moths

and now we admit defeat

     legs   upended in surrender   flat on our backs
       the last ears of wheat ripen   ruffled
       your golden silence
         is complete.

Mer De Glace

From the air it might be an alligator
mythical lizard born
of blizzard and ice, crocodile
snout nosing mile upon mile
of frozen mountain, back knobbled
crested with vertebrae moraines
tail flicking up the peaks
tongue dripping ice-melt
on homes in Chamonix below.

The rimy reptile was captured
in a monochrome
snapshot
freeze-framed
before snowfields
ice-filled seracs drained
before an emaciated glacier
beat a final retreat
before *Google Earth*
confirmed
we turned
our last dinosaur
into a pathetic
dribbling
worm.

Wolverine

Half lumbering badger,
half stubby bear
dressed for the worst
of a Finnish winter
you sing sad songs
of warm boreal Steppes

*

Restless stalker,
walker of Siberian wastes
fresh dead flesh is
your midnight nectar:
unwitting mink
fill your yawning whole.

*

Long night ranger,
curdle-blooded grubber,
meet me at the edge of the snow;
show me the colour
of wolverine love
before you go.

We Saw It All Happen

Just chilling   my family on a sofa
tucking into a *Deliveroo*
           got the zapper in my hands   channel trawling
prawn toast   popcorn calamari
               they're going down well

       and here's the new *One Planet*
although it started ages ago   catching it all
               on repeat

peeling back the wrapper on the tuna
the halibut's heated up

       I've got the zapper in my hand

watching the krill   go under
       icebergs   drift   away

       rumpus in the water   walruses
jostling for space

we're dipping into dishes   saltfish fritters
               clocking the walruses   heave their engines
       up a cliff

gripped by the flippers
how they haul tonnes of grunt   sluggy brains
               imagining supper   high above
the sharp rocks
               hungry flubber and tusk

got the zapper in my hands

but the picture doesn't change   those sea creatures
lugging themselves
                              up a cliff-face
food trays empty

        zapper pointing at the screen

those oily walruses   on the edge now
starting to topple
                        going over

        David's voice fails

                now we're all wailing
                kill the sound

blubber tumbling
through salty sky

got my zapper fixed on the screen   and no sound

                                walruses
in freefall now

                cartwheeling down the rocks

        killing time on the sofa   I'm killing

                I can't kill the sound

40

MAINS

Welcome To Hotel Extinction

A view to die for from any of our last resorts: whether remote island or sapphire lagoon, the outlook is unremittingly the same. We're frighteningly easy to travel to, our portfolio global. Another branch opens daily. Most guests are driven here. Many fly. All animals welcome. We apologise for the poor air conditioning. We guarantee a good sleep. Beware of a sudden proliferation in insects—rest assured we are committed to total elimination. Everything in the Ice Breaker Tavern is on the rocks, 24/7. We don't do a Happy Hour. Think Hotel California: check out any time you like but you can never leave. Daily wake-up calls are free. Sunset at the infinity pool is unforgettable. Every room always has flowers.

Five Degrees

Take one: another atoll gone, droughts, faster rate
of ice melt. Sweltering taxis. A few mortuaries fail
to cope in The Pyrenees. Chin up, it's not too late.

Two degrees: forget the Med. Instead, investigate
Aberystwyth for a tan. Gozo is a no-go. You can sail
across London in a skiff! Maybe the Earth's heart-rate

skips a beat. Three degrees. Now the floodgates
open. Holland (and the coral) gone. A large-scale
exodus from Africa. Geo-engineers arrive too late.

Work hard for a degree at Oxford-by-the-Sea, wait
for a Balliol boat. Bail out—Cambridge is a folktale.
At four, methane leaks from the sea floor, the rate

accelerates. Mangrove swamps, sapodillas create
new tropics in Paris. Bananas on a boulevard; so shale
had an upside after all. Take the fifth, way too late

to keep the lid on oceanic gas explosions so great
Hiroshima is but a flicker. Then the final coffin nail:
supercharged fireballs banging into cities at a rate
of knots. The lid lowers by degrees. Sorry: too late.

We Need Another Amazon

London Underground	*after morning showers*
commuters stand in lines	*scent of lotus flowers*
eyes bowed down	*in a tropical trance*
somewhere distant	*guardua bamboos dance*
umbrellas furled	*as if an exotic fern*
with leaves folded down	*had begun to burn*
when all along the platform	*like a gleaming ribbon*
passengers light up	*to a rainforest vision*
tannoys screech to life	*with cockatoo calls*
echoing parrots	*and hyacinth macaws*
while above the tracks	*ropes of heliconias*
their striped red shirts	*dangle lobster claws*
that cling in the heat	*emerge from the mist*
as the train arrives	*in an anaconda twist*
doors slide open	*onto lapunas, kapok trees*
a knot of twisted limbs	*tapirs rummaging in leaves*
then a voice in the distance	*somewhere in the blue*
cries *Mind The Gap*	*the world is falling through*

Driven To Extinction

Riding home in Dad's Capri after Herbie Rides Again
　　　　was a blizzard of insect wings,
smeared windscreen a grisly scene from *The Omen*.

Back then, our view of bugs was more Live And Let Die.
　　　　I would splurge my pocket money
on rubber dragonflies and spiders that made Cynthia cry.

We watched Starsky and Hutch to the deadened thump
　　　　of tiger moths blundering into windows,
scooped them in papery handfuls from a hurricane lamp.

Sunday mornings I'd sluice down the car for a fiver,
　　　　fish dead flies from the radiator grille:
beneath the foam, wounds of driving at night laid bare.

Now, Cinnabar moths are as rare as flares or a waterbed.
　　　　I drive home at nightfall through streets
marbled with light; the future clear as the road ahead.

Four Forms of Denial

[idle]

parked up in the four-by-four / like I'm just
chilling / outside the school gates / *like Heart
is on in the background* / *maybe it was Magic* /
or Heat / and it was dropping off the children
time / like just keeping myself warm / engine
pumping out heat / like just a few particles
don't kill / mums and children outside the gates
/ not like they were inhaling / just the odd
like particle / *it was Smooth* / *no maybe it was
Heart* / and I swear the kids weren't breathing
in fumes / not like it was asthma / *like was
it Heart* / *or Smooth* / *maybe it was like Magic*

[CARNIVORE]

ISN'T IT ABOUT SURVIVAL   A PRIMAL URGE
NATURAL HUNTER GATHERER INSTINCTS
AND CHRISTMAS   WOULDN'T BE CHRISTMAS
WITHOUT THE FLESH AND BLOOD SO WHAT
IF WE DON'T CARE   FOR OFFAL OR INNARDS
WHAT BE A GORILLA   ONLY EVER EAT FRUIT
AND NUTS   IT'S NOT LIKE CAVEMEN DINED
ON CASHEWS MARINATED TOFU JUST TAKE
ESKIMOS' PERFECT TEETH   CHEW ON THAT

[personal]

you don't do hooves
you do salamino tofu
choose beet blush brie
instead of cheese
your pores leach Quorn
you ditched prawn crisps
for *Pig Out Chips*
you knock back
black pepper shots
you've climbed on board
ready for take off

[PRESIDENTIAL]

IF PLANTS COULD VOTE   THEY'D VOTE FOR COAL
WE NEED TO START A FIRE   USE A BIG FAT DOSE
OF CLEAN AND BEAUTIFUL NATURAL GAS   GOOD
FOR MANKIND IF THIS WORLD GETS ANY KINDER
IT'S LITERALLY GOING TO CEASE TO EXIST   YOU
DON'T NEED MONEY TO FIGHT WILD FIRES WHAT
YOU SEE AND READ   IS NOT WHAT'S HAPPENING

Global Warming
(A lipogram)

Mallow ill in a loggia, a marginal growl,
a low moan. Algal alarm, a wan
bog, a blown worm on a lawn,
lamb born in a binbag. A ragbag lion,
animal agonal. A growing nag.
A liana growing in limbo, worn
rainbow, abnormal rain. An albino
gorilla aglow, a moralling aria, largo.
A long low moan, a wrong aroma,
a glaring oilman in brawling garb.
Malign lingo. Wonga mania, grim loam.
A glib million gambling on oil, a raging
mob blaming granola or a long ago
Big Bang. Raw war: no win, no air.

Alberta's Story

Like all of them they oiled their words with promises;
in those early days they came with slurry blenders,

equipment that pumped at staggering pressure.
Proppants deployed, backed up with explosive fluids

to get in *real deep*, to breach cracks in the deepest
formations of rock. Hydraulic fracturing agents

pinned the tight chalks open until gases streamed out.
We felt the vein-filled shale split beneath us – seismic,

it rattled every disc in our spines. Too many stresses
triggered miniature earthquakes; with one awkward thrust

connate waters flooded through subterranean chambers,
every rib split as hydrochloric acid flushed out vital fibre.

In the mornings we woke to foul lakes of tailings, viscous
aggregates of metal: zirconium, antimony, titanium salts.

When the earth stopped moving, our hollowed-out bodies
were blasted: bones rattle like matchsticks, every cough

froths with toxic sand. It took only one unguarded frack
to contaminate our lifeblood, to turn all our rivers black.

Mammoth
(to Big Oil)

You barrelled across the Earth like you owned it
        and to a degree or two you did.
        Too big to fail,
                the world hitched a ride on your matted back.

Your footfall left prints wide as opencast mines,
        while you, grass guzzler,
        masticated mammoth
           amounts of habitat to fuel your unstoppable growth.

Those manipulative tusks tore into foes.
        You thundered over steppes,
        plundered deltas,
           leaving behind a bitumen stink of oily tailings.

Maa mutt, *earth mole,* too entrenched too in your ways—
        now you're obsolete
        as a page of Green Shield Stamps.
           Fields you once roamed over rolled into foamy acres

under the North Sea. Now we unearth rig-like ribcages,
        bones which further the notion
        you drove yourself
           to extinction, clumsy species that limbered up too late.

Mammoth, you should have shaken off your crude pelt
        before the ice melted.
        Thick-skinned galumpher,
           you failed to acclimatise to the change in the tide.

Burning Rubber

Here soft-tread desert is remoulded
        into smouldering black forest, slate landscape
                of hollowed-out rubber, well-worn lava erupted

from an explosion in man-made waste—
        dark oasis in an Emirate for tyres that have lost
                their grip, dead that outnumber the living

by three to one. Countless cars passed
        under stars to get here: ribbed and lugged,
                their tyres undulate under an unforgiving sun

like waves in the windless heat, redundant
        as husk from nuts. Instead of making compost
                they combust, release pungent essential oils,

swirling blends of precipitated silica and rubber.
        Plumes of smoke billow across endless desert:
                a choking canopy, ghost of a million trees.

Folding Green

When the hedgies moved in, they dumped old bonds,
        went long on conglomerates, short on anything in rows,
anything skittish, scuttling or moving in a sideways trend.

In came the runners of funds, the pumpers and dumpers,
        fixers and riggers until fly-by-night capital took fright.
Out flew the featherbedded assets, flippers, floaters,

assorted gold bugs, lame ducks all sold down the river
        by passive investors until lifetime creepers shifted
operations offshore. Too many gambles on futures,

murky safe havens were left high and dry. Fish turned
        phishers, pikes became pikers, hawks swished into doves.
One lone shark stayed the same. The banks collapsed,

swathes of distressed assets no longer recession-proof.
        All that remained: an empty liquidity trap, a downward
butterfly curve. Naturally the vulture funds swooped—

sudden spikes in trading as they plumped for cattle
        and live hogs. Swipe through FT Online and you'll find
every stock always plunges again by the closing bell.

Green Wash

TIP A CAPFULL OR TWO
ONTO ANY SOILED GOODS

THIS URGENT DETERGENT FRESHENS EMISSIONS

SOFT-SOAP YOUR OILS!

NO BAD CORPORATE ODOURS AT ALL

BUSINESS AS USUAL spun
into *MAXIMISING OUR
POSITIVE IMPACT*

EVERY REVOLUTION = MORE
FLUFF AND FLANNEL!

EFFICACIOUS ON THE MOST INGRAINED INDUSTRIAL STAINS!

TRANSITIONS YOUR BITUMENS

HOT-WASH YOUR OFF-SHORES AND ORES!

ENDLESSLY RECYCLABLE!

DIAPHANOUS FROTH!

EVEN THE FILTHIEST OUTFIT FLUFFS UP SOFTER THAN A LONG-FORGOT-TEN ARCTIC WINTER!

WITH ADDED LAVENDER

TO SAVE THE PLANET!

WARNING: THIS PRODUCT IS CORROSIVE IF SWALLOWED

Polcevera

Your silent storm was building for years,
a five-decade span of deliberate laxness
taking its toll. We noticed it in the whiplash
of broken cables beating against bared ribs,
a *correttore* of botched repairs to conceal
hints of age, shoddy clothes riddled with holes
and authorities who chose to *chiudere un occhio*.

I crossed you once; the distress was palpable:
the length of your body trembled, knuckles
white as you struggled to keep a grip, smile
overstretched, sagging like worn-out elastic.
How could you hold yourself together in public
while beneath, weakened by a scandalous state
of neglect, your stricken heart was about to break?

Starbucks In The Gutter

Down with the dandelions,
legs sprawled across dirt, he's down
on his uppers with sod all
but a hold-all, a drizzle of old coppers,
a used coffee cup.

Ground down, down at heel, he's worn
down to the bare leather
stitches of his sole. Horizons glimpsed
through sticky plastic lids, the envy
of a warm sip of latte,

coughs of muttered pleases,
ravenous for any small change.
For this is what he is:
flat, tight, a Costa cup on his knees,
a sloshed dosser in need

of a top-up, for a shot of sympathy.
Chucked in the gutter,
his stars are buckled, fucked up,
while we cradle the stain
of a disposable cup in our hands.

Lockdown Sonnets

1. The Fish
(after Elizabeth Bishop)

Huge shoals had already converged
in waters offshore, governments insisting
it was far too soon to go trawling
even though we were already at sea, certain
of a tremendous haul. Hand-gelled
and double-gloved we set full sail
on a Pomegranate Tide, headed for isles
spritzed with a bracing Citrus Kelp.
What a baleful catch we made,
the deck flailing and flapping with covids
until someone detected the curious fish
were afflicted. We sprayed and sprayed
until everything was *Dettol, Dettol, Dettol!*
and then we let the fish go.

2.   Saffron Green

I discovered it on a run, something
I'd never done before, exploring
the richer world hidden beyond
the front door. Pasture turned
into woodland until it was layer
upon layer of primrose, anemone
paths tickled with white comfrey,
finches in trees, just inches away
from the A1. I watched the conceit
of exhausted lives in the fast lane
rush by, the tang of arcane
carbon in its wake, now obsolete
as packed tubes or nine to five
and I was astounded to be alive.

3.   I Found A Bluebell Wood

How to capture that full watery
brilliance, the surround-sound of fitful
birdsong: it was as if the whole of April
was running off an overcharged battery.
More at home under a moon than sun,
low blue flames rose from leafy debris,
a temporary show for locked-down weeks,
campions offsetting the sober tone.
Never were so many bells silent at once:
a congregation of flowers at prayer
while we prayed for the dying elsewhere,
on wards the colour of those Spanish hyacinths
by stealth invading the countryside
while the woods bathed in stained glass light.

4.   The Great Plague Of London

So many similarities: a tricksy pox
incubated in animals, its sneaky manner
of hitching a ride on the back of travellers
pattering along the Silk Road, folk
of the better sort* getting the hell
out of the capital to an upscale
pied-à-terre on the outskirts of Bath …
but the most macabre parallel
is with plague searchers, women tasked
like Goodwife Hubble, tuppence a corpse
for hurried rummages and scribbled records
of death. No gels or protective masks,
just themselves grappling with loved ones.
Ecclesiastes: nothing is new under the sun

*Daniel Defoe *A Journal Of The Plague Year*

5.   Rush Hour

One month in and a wild rush hour
quickened along the verges, nature
slamming down hard on the accelerator,
rigs of cow parsley towered
over kerbs in Galley Lane, exploding
into stars, rivers of bluebells lapped
against the tarmac on a surge of sap
fuelled by a million lost springs.
Dandelions had no time to turn clocks
into ashes when the lockdown stopped.
Air charged with birdsong soured
in the roar of a more familiar rush hour
when strimmers returned to crew-cut
the verges, all the new rivers dried up.

6. Una Fodera Argento

When the clouds cleared we spied an upside,
a silver lining said some. In the streets
our lungs began to breathe more freely,
a sliver of blue sky for those who survived.
In Venice, canals flowed Murano-blue,
beneath the Rialto they were translucent
as cristallo glass, a clear-cut solution
to *la problema continuo di inquinamento,*
continual pollution. Some breathed
better while others breathed their last,
a retreating tide of greenhouse gases
neutralised by a surge in those bereaved.
Una fodera d'argento to the virus,
my God, it came at a price.

Caterpillar

The weeks play out in peaks and troughs
        charted by the parabola of his back.
He meanders from one room to another,
        all wreathed in the same leafy wallpaper.
Every morsel of groundsel is a Groundhog Day.
        There's no furlough for a hungry caterpillar.

He knows an airborne killer hovers over
        his world of constant foraging, a beak
swooping out from behind the green curtain.
        One day his restricted life will be lifted
by the gods gifting him a pair of wings.
        From the cockpit of his modified body,
he will gaze down goggle-eyed on a land
        reconfigured, where for a few precious weeks
heaven was a place of herbal teas, perpetual eating
        garden meals the boundaries of liberation.

Where will his new-found freedom take him?

Hypersonic Gods

The old gods did their damage and moved on
save for the more vengeful ones
circulating in a firmament where every star is
armed. With names to match
the ancients: *Avangard, Dark Eagle, Zircon*,
they dodge other gods, track
the earth's curve to lock onto their quarry,

travelling in chariots emblazoned
with stars unconstrained by laws of physics.
Propelled by batteries and rockets
they bear payloads that throb with hypersonic
thunderbolts forged in ungodly
smithies, to be hurled down at five times
the speed of sound. Ruthless

and brutal, like ancient deities they're bent
on retribution. A single finger
could blast the ancient Pyramids to bits.
Below them, snow is no longer
immortal, the Arctic an island on a rising tide,
and lesser gods in their own orbits
press on, intent on their own destruction.

Celandines and Blue Sky

(A poem for Ukraine)

Rootstock like weathered knuckles, they dig in deep,
       resilient against
            bitter easterlies,
unflinching through the winter's rubble. Disturb one

when turning over permeable earth and suddenly
       they're everywhere,
            tubers re-rooting
inches away from their mothers. However exact

the attack, each year their gold flowers come back,
       reliable as stars
            and solar-powered,
as if the sun were shivered into sharp showers.

For weeks they amaze, low flames blazing like May,
       with snowdrops
            barely in their graves,
to fight relentless battles against tougher invaders,

ground elder or thistles determined to claim new turf.
       Blood-tipped,
             thick-set thistles
bristle with ill intent, guided only by the fractured logic

of their heads. Oblivious to neat borders, perennials
       with rusting heads
            rain down mayhem
until their offspring shoot out tap-roots like iron spikes,

shoving aside feebler weeds. After Spring has sucked
      the celandines dry,
            their silent sirens
sound loud enough to fill a summer of roaring skies.

Norilsk

is built on frosted bones   of Gulag prisoners
bodies preserved   beneath black slag heaps
stunted birches   endless mud. The only way
in or out   through air deadened by sulphur
belched out by a nickel smelter   *Nadezhda*
whose name means *hope*.   On its rusted sign
someone crossed out the name.   Foraging
for wild food here is forbidden. The sun fails
to rise in winter over a hill they call *Golgotha*.

Whiplash winds   batter Soviet tower blocks
forcing residents to cower indoors.   On days
without gales   freezing smog licks windows
warmer winds from the Arctic   find a way in
loosening foundations   built on permafrost
Nadezhda wobbles   a blood vessel ruptures
tons of diesel   bleed into the *Ambarnaya*
polar river running crimson as Autumn leaves.
In Summer   people go swimming in the lake.

Changeling

my nature changed
my moods monsooned   I cast spells of rain
wept ice melt
          swept by tropical depressions
my skin fracked   organs fragmented
my hives were left empty

spring brought a new start
each one sooner than the last   by June my chestnut hair
withered with blight
          houses blazed in my wake
dust devils danced   wildflowers turned to rape
bees supplanted by drones

there was no quick switch
no single trade   but a slow sea change
tides edged higher
          my mouth became a swollen river
flotsam hardened to plastic   discarded fish
silvered my heatwaves

sceptics rubbished me
labelled me *a myth*   ignored the trickle
of microbeads
          into basins where I washed
a slow-building catastrophe   inexorable drift
to no snow

now I caress chimney breasts
sleep on their grates   primed by firelighters
to fly up the flue
contorted in a bawl of flame
nothing left   but a pyroclastic cloud
of hex and ash.

Mortal

I was born maroon snakeroot
　　　　haemorrhage a black septic sap
so lock up your hoverflies
　　　　from my Venus Flytrap.
I am skullcap, dogtooth,
　　　　maunch on a corncockle salad
masticate wolfsbane,
　　　　tallow tree, mad maladies
of blind beggar's tick. I don
　　　　a devil's helmet to prong
a belladonna, dumb cane
　　　　poke with a fungry hound's tongue
gropecherry, cockhold,
　　　　vape a viper's bugloss
blue, itch for the leather hide
　　　　of a fiddle-leaf fig, floss
with a jimson weed knot.
　　　　I fish the twisted depths
of a fruity fool's funnel
　　　　extract prophylactics
for psychotropic gruels; thickened
　　　　with cuckoo pint and spit from a fit
I am Jack of the Pulpit
　　　　I should not be picked.

Plastic Rain

We never asked where the souls of old bottles went,
those disposable empties thrown on the waves.

Some matured in the ocean's cellars, others ascended
into the firmament to be swallowed by clouds

and then spat out. Clouds containing rain became rain
clouded by containers. It began to bucket down.

The first downpour was at sea, bottles torpedoed
into churned up waves. No one blinked when

a million washed up on beaches the next day.
Drizzle over cities turned to a bottle cap patter,

scattered across roofs like pennies from heaven.
Flytippers complained about competition from the rain.

Showers became Instagrammable, blue and green
bead curtains hung from clouds. Gutters in deadbeat suburbs

looked more or less the same. One night a thunderstorm
pounded London, Sodastream lightning, bottles flying

like a riot. In summer, drifts of single-use snow
refused to melt. And a child could touch a rainbow.

We Crave a Sea Change

the chance to cure, to chart a courageous course,
a check on chasing conspicuous consumption,
for craven, cheating companies to be curtailed.
We challenge the charlatans, the criminally corrupt,

the cavalier creeps and their cynical cronies
without conscience in the Commons. We covet
a closing of chapters, a complete cessation
to congestion, the curse of crushed commutes,

to all the catastrophic causes of climate change.
We call for a cessation to counting on crude,
on coal-mines and cars, to the contemptible
contamination of coral and crops. We clamour

for closer cooperation, creation of a common centre,
confident but cautious, we champion a countryside
of cowslips and clover, conservation of all
its creepy-crawlies. No caveats, we need to see change.

Avocado

I cradle you
in my palms, press
my thumbs *like this* upon your skin.
See how the sinews begin to loosen,
the telling softness of your flesh
as you begin to give. A couple of cuts
through leather reveal your splendour:
the creamy meat, its buttery flavour,
muted bitterness, a hint of lust.
But take your kernel, see how it slips
through my fingers, falls to the floor.
A faraway love gnaws at your core,
your kisses sit too distant on my lips.
O flighty lover, how can I discard
the small warm planet
of your heart?

AFTERS

At The Ice House

Polished mahogany tables overflowed
under the weight of Regency treats:
calves' foot jellies, sweetmeats,
wobbling flummery ambrosial

on concealed ice-beds, hand-harvested
from Norwegian fjords. Numb-thumbed
cutters, slicing through rime, fashioned
breeze-blocks of ice to fit

into steamships, sawdust-stuffed
to stave off melt, cargoes stowed
between beams of deal below,
cubes cracked big enough

to fill the pyramid of Khufu.
Staring now into the brick-lined
void unearthed in grounds behind
a stuccoed row, it hits you

how a division of spoils is where it begins:
with the convivial aristocratic clack
of a vintage hock or an *Escubac*
on the rocks, how tickling a gentleman's

gins counts more to those in power
than the cost of a frosted bourbon,
how so many only ever reflect on
melting ice when it is raised in a tumbler.

Eton Mess

Meringue and cream, all lightness and fluff, topped with a juicy promise.

A void within a vacuum surrounded by a vast inanition.
nihil-ad-rem

Can be cobbled together in seconds.

- First take the meringue (white) break it in with cream (also white).
- Crush the strawberries until the pips squeak and the juices run like blood.
- Mash. Scrummy!
- Aterthought: sprinkle with spun sugar (for decoration).

No deep thought or application required.

NB *nota bene*: some of the ingredients demand prodigious wealth.
(Yep, they'll cost you.)

> Like all of them, best served chilled.
> Dust conservatively with icing sugar (or cocaine).

A great final flourish after you've made a greased pig's ear of the main!

(Snaffle in chambers between divs)

Oh Sugar!

It was only a year after the Temporary Emergency Authorisation Order that it began. A bride sliced into a three-tier wedding cake, guests were treated to cake teeming with deceased blister beetles and leaf-hoppers, hard to tell apart from candied peel. Reports came in that Mr Kipling cakes were laced with dead aphids, bodies of spider mites solidified inside fruit pastilles. Packets of sweets were little more than body bags of bugs. Pots of jam swam with corpses of preserved army worms, marmalade contained jellified shreds of crickets suspended like ants in amber. Brown marmorated stink bugs pitched up in ketchup, poisoned bees swarmed in litres of Lucozade, fizzing as if they were still alive. People started dropping like flies: small quantities won't *kill* you! insisted the Authorities. Although farmers carried on planting fields of the immaculate but calamitous crops, they knew that they were beat.

Fatberg

It might have escaped from a laboratory:
 a biological curiosity
  with the body of an octopus
   but no limbs, a pudgy
    limpid belly, jellified cheeks
     and bulging condom eyes
     with a *Double Decker* wrapper
    for a tongue. The flushers
   discovered its mother
 snoozing in Whitechapel's bowels
swaddled in a blanket of fat
 a recumbent stalagmite
  of discarded wet wipes
   bringing London's movements to a halt.

   Now a gang of riveted children
    gasp at a quivering sliver
    caged behind strengthened glass
   as it spawns an army of small flies
  and wonder at the perversity
 of a monstrous sculpture
carved out of our own bodies,
 a disgusting portrayal in oils
  of a terrible time of waste.

Cotton Buds

i

you roll
us across
antihelical
folds
drive us
deeper
into your
navicular
fossa
umbilicus
until we're
a wound
& dressing
blessing
& scourge
woolly-
headed
products
of your
fondness
for
polish

ii

soft-
tipped
cotton-
wick
matchsticks
slicked
in cochlear
wax
infinitely
flexible
dibbles
we're the
pick-up
sticks
birthing
rituals
of furbishing
babies
outliving
each
new
born

iii

why do
you pick
on us
fractions
of plastic
facial
probes
fabricated
to excavate
wax-
locked
lobes
plucked
from
a box
of pastel
candles
to mark
a century
being
thrown
away

iiii

double-
budded
we never
burgeon
or decay
when
you cast
us aside
we become
rictus
grins
for fish
braids
for
seahorse
tails
earth's
eternal
pink
&
blue
veins

Lyrical On Wax

&

lo

it came to pass that to mark the end of the world
they lit a million candles; while the Earth burned
they   turned   to   *Aubèrpine* and *Cannelle,* dipped
their strings into vats of boiling wax redolent of
freshly-laundered   linen,   the hot stench of scalded
blouses filled their houses while the Earth burned.
They   turned   to   the charms of *Pine   Needle*, *Yuzu
Rose*,   *Goji   Tarocco,* the air a hazy *Ambre Lumiere*
until   even   the   pomegranates ran to *Blood & Noir*,
Fucking   Fabulous they screamed, *More & More,
Spicy Forests*   turned to ashes as the Earth burned.
They converted aspens into matches, filled a room
with   *Golden Feu De Bois* and the scent of burning
Angels Wings. In winter, they fired up a *Sparkling
Frost,* watched as their *Snow In Love* melted, until
the *Starry   Starry Nights* and *Homes Sweet Homes* were
no more, no more than a pool of hardening wax
on a table laid bare   all while the Earth burned.

Off The Map

only a spit left

        slobber of sand

              in a sunburned ocean

drool

             gob of atoll

slice of paradise   diced

             into scum and phlegm

    coughed up by firestorm

             froth of surge

      churned to a fury

Hurricane Walaka   incandescent

      boiled over   hot seas

opened up *kālani*

        devoured

green turtle hatchlings   monk seal pups   albatrosses
but no white dove

      the hurricane never hesitated

pounded Hawaii

    gouged out an isle   East Island

    finger of dry land   raised a white flag

      dislocated bone

        bare rib of sea

    dismembered

             a memory

two thousand years

shattered into shoals
   rags   a hole

    archipelago of words

 erased from the page

gone

Ocean Autopsy

We unwrapped her from the matted
        plastic that covered her for decades,
her oil-slicked body of water mutilated

        face criss-crossed by shipping lanes,
briny tears on her cheeks. Sinkhole skin,
        sunken ship of her lips mouthing *no, no.*

We made a wave-shaped slit, delta
        to continental shelf, blubber abscissioned
to expose over-fished ribs. Stench of dead

        shark-fall, bone-eating worms crawling
from abyssopelagic layer. Signs of muscles
        wasted, corals bleached. And then deep

into trenches of the chest to vital organs,
        gallbladder wracked with tangled weed,
gullets and inlets obstructed with netting.

        The heart of her was darkness, graveyard
of amphipods, cold seeps, hydrothermal vents.
        Her sea stars snuffed out, one by one.

Last, the Hadal Zone of her cranium, over-trawled
        pathways indicative of a glacier-cracked brain,
every sign of life evaporated. Possible causes

        of death: suffocation, signs of homicide.
When they send her to the grave, there'll be
        little left to bury but a hollowed-out shell.

Little Whirlpool Ramshorn Snail

A name twenty times its length, curled
on a page indexing threatened species,
smaller even than a waterboatman's oar
pushed out to the fringes of extinction.

These water specks, scaled-down ammonites,
translucent on the edge of a Sussex ditch,
crawl among the marginals, dodging carp
to clamp onto reeds they still call home.

Despite the incursion, the plucky Ramshorns
cling on, skim ditches for scraps of algae,
flattened whorls spiralling ever further down
through the ferny fringes of a marshy nook.

Small coils that spin in a run-down clock,
man's hands have been moving against them,
conchologists wading in to their rescue,
trying to wind the miniature cogs back.

Drought Stress

Shrivelled leaves confetti the dirt path,
starved and ridged, a twisted crocodile's back.

Bare roots protrude like ribs through skin,
spring sludge corrugated into clefts and rifts.

Under bare skies, ants pause at crumbling gorges
that once were mud; a dragonfly alights on a gully.

Soft clays of May turned to August dust,
fallen blossoms of hawthorn rust on the ground.

Let swallows fly lower, clover close up,
rain swell the veins of the woods again

gutters river, mosses wallow in bogs, earth
opens up its throat, swallow a rainbow whole.

Let the whole damned sky thunder-crack,
fingers of lightning pierce clouds into showers,

ease through damp folds of leaves to a place
where small-eyed flowers can breathe.

Divorce Hearing

It is our position that this marriage
was of unequals, which is to say
one side brought the wealth:

> silver-plated armadillo, gilded
> lily flame, bronze-winged wren,
> mother-of-pearl dusted snow

while the other was oafish,
unschooled, ill-equipped, feverish
eyes fixed on his squalid nest

> this marriage of convenience,
> unholy from the very beginning,
> has reached a tipping point

a pivotal point of no return,
where all that has been lost:
Pyrenean Ibex, Stellers Sea Cow,

> Passenger Pigeon, Great Auk
> (which I concede some may consider
> losses of minor consequence)

has begun to undermine
this relationship's foundation,
soured the very air

> made it impossible for both parties
> to co-exist; *m'lud* let us not
> seek to apportion any blame

but to split the spoils of a marriage
where one side ran wild while
the other pushed the wild aside

      let us seek a fair settlement
      where one party receives cash
      the other the vacated property

sea lapping against the sills,
bare boards riddled with worm,
rafters exposed to baking sun.

Lamezia Terme

Beach tesselated with drifts

of burnt plants, wisps of dull

thrift, ghosts of verbascum,

buckthorn, storm-rocked kale

sickle-shaped pods. Spider-

headed spiniflex whisked

across silver-shingle grains

by wind like fists

on a red-hot hob. Sea-oat,

gorse, every salt-crisped shrub

on its knees, sits in ash flicked

from its own rigid stub.

Wailing plovers in jagged

lines scour pulverized shells

glittering among a litter

of charred cars, plastic bottles.

Big O
(i.m.)

He was crude, spewed more damn filth
than a fracking pipeline flowback,
never tell the truth when a good lie'll do.

Full-on Boss Hogg, those Texan hands
could fix a bell nipple faster than shit
through a critter, drink the blue ass off

an Alabama slammer bar in a night.
Black day when Ol' King Coal got shot,
but then the kill-line for Big O kicked in

when the whole darn world locked down.
Plugs ruptured, his blowout preventer
got plain plumb-tuckered. Sour gas

spudded through his limbs, black holes
at his heart laid bare. Dude so fracking
frail, goddam wind blown him clean away.

Hope Is A Thing With Tubers

coarse offspring of mustard   crossed with common vetch
        our engineered limbs
                herd oily seepings
into roots of gloomy catacombs   honeydew folds of polymers

we salivate for the zing of kerosene   slugs of dirty diesel
        sulphurous gasps
             from foul-mouthed mines
the croaky halitosis of engines revved   tarmac touch-downs

our carbon-hungry corridors   tar-furred
        with iodide residues
            smoke-rings from smelted ores
that twist through our fissures   to dilate the Earth's veins

our genius is to bottle them   to cap the poisonous saps
        juices of spent fuels
           stoppered
in corky rootstocks   until the Earth cools

one day you may quarry us
dig us out   black as slack

      then you will learn what it means
           for history to repeat itself

witness again   what it means
          to burn.

When It Came To Ways Of Saving The Planet

we were ears, all ears,
auricles cocked, cochlears entirely attentive

we were concentrated cartilage, auditory, alert,
the body's tiniest chambers

reverberating to fervent predictions
of defrosted glaciers, forest fires.

Goggle-eared receptors,
we were one collective listening post

no climate revelation evaded us,
warning words clattered down eustachian tubes

into an internal induction loop,
anvils and hammers chiming in time

our ears equipped with adequate bandwidth
to harbour a thousand cities submerged

beneath water, enough tympanic cavities
to contain every garden emptied of butterflies.

So many words lost in labyrinthine whorls,
we couldn't hear the woods for the trees.

Considering My Footprint

The fruit bowl is a problematic city of pineapple
        skyscrapers, a maze of apricot alleys, banana
dead ends. Whenever I'm hungry I lose my footing,

        skate over unseasonal strawberries from Spain
but the grapes are moonscape, a pebbly beach
        to negotiate. Every peach is seaside at low tide,

lines of footprints marking each year it rises higher.
        Slippery banana inclines peel away to reveal
a delicate tightrope between mouth and tree.

        I circumnavigate *Braeburns* with ease, *Pink Ladies*
are more problematic. Blueberries are squeezy scree,
        my feet leave prints in their glaucous wax.

I cross the soft bomb of a pomegranate; like pineapples,
        I'm aware of potential shrapnel. Watermelons
are giant grenades, too perilous to contemplate.

        I brave walking barefoot over an avocado,
my feet scorch on the pulpy lava of its flesh,
        the hard heart of its magma boiling at the core.

I leave a trail like wet morning grass, wounds
        and indentations that spread until the whole
fruit bowl turns indigo, darkening to a bruise.

Guerrilla

I'm declaring war from the border
I'm raising an army of stubborn weeds
tarmac's on the attack   and I want my land back

so I'm taking up arms against asphalt
agitating against wasted space
got a pocket full of wildflower seeds
and I'm blowing up the hard shoulders
the banks are in my sights

it's raining down loosestrife
wild rocket's landing on kerbs
weeds hit the dirt
these daisies are armed   and dangerous
I want a new revolution in the lanes

buttercups firing up the gutters
ragged robins running riot
hounds-tongues trashing a roundabout
the hogweed's smoking   on a broken white line

to a soundtrack of bugles,
choirs of yellow archangels
my corncockles in full cry

I don't want roads I want clover
I want thyme   I want thrift
trench warfare against the endless drives
and your big wheels won't stop us

until irises run up a white flag
until I see heartsease   honesty

and love lies bleeding
by every wasted roadside

I'm Hooked On The Jellyfish Live Cam

They rise like smoke in a windless winter,
        descend with the languor of summer,
yet they're a slow-motion spring, budding

        and unfurling their tangerines and yellows,
petals billowing around translucent coronas.
        Never falling to earth, they berth themselves

in water, each shift a slow-motion ecstasy,
        an opening and closing of lips, those seductive
tentacles less soft cotton than electric fences,

        hard-wired to stun an oblivious sunfish.
They sleep as they wake in a dream state,
        bodiless souls floating in permanent limbo

across the world's shifting sands. Noiseless,
        yet surely they sound a low note: mellow,
a Chet Baker solo, chords long held and lost.

        Who wouldn't envy those who glissade
through life like this, oblivious to the tide, unburdened
        by flesh, feathered by pillows of undertow

only to be caught in the arms of themselves?
        Slowed-down meteors, they're more space
than matter, streaming not venom but peace.

        Away from the screen, they stay with you,
waxing and waning like rainbows in the mind,
        shape-shifting the spirit into self-reflection

all tops and tails, no eyes yet all eyes, they cast
        no shadows, no more than light streaming through
the highest rose window in the cathedral of the sea.

Flip The Track

bring the old school back - Montell Jordan, from *Club Classics*

Let's get it on, start to dance again. Eat more veggies
        then don't stop til you get enough. More more more!
Feel the pulses pumping, don't blame it on the boogie.

Plump for less beef, let those artichoke hearts run free.
        The beets go on and on and on with vegan spanakopita,
so rock the boat with a cauli, a hot pot of chili non carne.

Breed less. It's a tragedy but rein in the men. It's ladies'
        night and the time is right, got to give it up. People all over
the world, join in. Can you feel it? Blame it on the boogie.

High NRG? Ooh baby it's coal outside and only electricity
        when you kiss me. Feel the force of a solar-powered car.
Burnt the house down, now we're picking up the pieces.

Hit me with green technologies, stayin' alive being thrifty.
        Dim all the lights, dance in the moonlight. It's night fever
and that's the way I like it, aha? Blame it on the boogie

because this is what it sounds like when doves cry: boogie
        oogie oogie no more. Disco's an inferno, each day another
one bites the dust. La, la, la, now we're picking up the pieces.
        Just don't blame it on the sunshine. Or the boogie.

Ash

My heart has darkening rings about it
age has carved its name on my bark;
limbs creak, l sway on a stick
it's hard to see stars in the dark.
But the years fail to stem my ambition
of one day taming the sun. I imagine
a tangle of branches extending a cage
around Earth, like fish in a coral cave.
Forests would follow, in a mass revolution
of leaves, a green solution to pollution,
where the branch and bough join hands
to encase the globe in a protective blanket.
A desperate last gasp to save the planet,
I want the world to warm to my plan.

About the Author

Julian Bishop has had a lifelong interest in ecology thanks largely to a childhood in rural Wiltshire. He's a former television journalist and apart from poetry has a passion for gardens, running and dogs, although not necessarily in that order. He lives with his family in North London.

Previous Publications

Lobster was awarded runner-up prize in the 2018 International Ginkgo Prize

Pangolin was runner-up in the 2020 Ver Poets Competition

Highlights Of Mining For Gold was published by The Alchemy Spoon, (Spring 2022)

The Last Giraffe was published by Ink Sweat and Tears, Autumn 2021

Snow Leopard was published by Words For The Wild, Autumn 2021

To The Man Who Poisoned 420 Eagles In A Year was published in the second *Voices For The Silent* anthology for the League Against Cruel Sports (Indigo Dreams Press) July 2022

Dung Beetles was a finalist in the Beaver Trust Eco-Poetry Competition 2021

At A Ceremony To Mark A Million Ways To Drive Small Creatures To Extinction featured in the second issue (Winter 2020) of The Alchemy Spoon

Mer De Glace was a featured poem in Enfield's Big Green Festival 2021

Wolverine was commended in the Ver Poets Ten-Liners Competition 2020

Welcome To Hotel Extinction was published by Briefly Write in December 2021

Five Degrees will be published in Magma Poetry in their Schools magazine issue Spring 2023

Mortal was published in The Dawn Treader (Indigo Dreams Press) Summer 2019

At The Ice House was published in the *Dear Politicians* anthology curated by Helen Moore Autumn 2022

Eton Mess was published by Tentacular magazine, Autumn 2022.

Global Warming was published by 14 Magazine, October 2022

Alberta's Story was published by Poetry Village, June 2020

Mammoth was published by Consilience Journal, November 2021

Folding Green was published in the UK's Morning Star daily newspaper, July 2020

Polcevera was published in the first issue of The Alchemy Spoon, July 2020

Starbucks In The Gutter was runner-up in the 2020 Aryamati Prize, Fly On The Wall Press

Saffron Green was published by Climate Cultures, September 2020 climatecultures.net

I Found A Bluebell Wood was published by Dust Magazine, Issue 6, *Glimmer,* January 2021

Caterpillar featured in The Fife Contemporary Art Festival, 2021

Changeling was published by Green Ink Poetry for their Pyres issue, August 2021

Fatberg was displayed by The Museum Of London as part of an exhibition on fatbergs

Little Whirlpool Ramshorn Snail was published by Magma Poetry in their Anthropocene issue, 2021

Drought Stress was published by Finished Creatures, Spring 2022

Divorce Hearing was published in Finished Creatures, Issue Three, Spring 2020

Lamezia Terme was published by Fly On The Wall Poetry, December 2020

When It Came To Ways Of Saving The Planet was published by Orbis magazine, Autumn 2022

I'm Hooked On The Jellyfish Live Cam was commended in the Troubadour Prize 2021.

Ash was published by The Writers' Café August 2018

NOTES

For Starters: Temperatures above 100F may have caused a mass die-off of mussels in California, *The Guardian, June 2019*

Poached Salmon: videos filmed in Oregon in 2019 and again in 2021 showed salmon dying because the river became too hot, *KGW News and Columbia Riverkeeper via YouTube*

Remember When Hippos Used To Swim? Story and photographs reported on *greenworldwarriors.com, September 2019*

Highlights of Mining for Gold in Indonesia: Headline from the website of Baru Gold Corp

Sulawesi Warty Pigs: Archaelogists discovered a 45,000-year-old Indonesian cave painting of now endangered pigs, *BBC January 2021*

Snow Leopard: A snow leopard was shot dead at Dudley Zoo after escaping in November 2018, *BBC*

To The Man Who Poisoned 420 Eagles In A Year: an Australian farmer was jailed and fined for the killings at Tubbut in east Gippsland, *ABC News, September 2018*

Dung Beetles: could vanish within a century, *Biological Conservation Journal, February 2019*

About Fly on the Wall Press

A publisher with a conscience.
Political, Sustainable, Ethical.
Publishing politically-engaged, international fiction, poetry and cross-genre anthologies on pressing issues. Founded in 2018 by founding editor, Isabelle Kenyon.

Some other publications:

The Woman With An Owl Tattoo by Anne Walsh Donnelly
The Prettyboys of Gangster Town by Martin Grey
The Sound of the Earth Singing to Herself by Ricky Ray
Inherent by Lucia Orellana Damacela
Medusa Retold by Sarah Wallis
Pigskin by David Hartley
We Are All Somebody
Aftereffects by Jiye Lee
Someone Is Missing Me by Tina Tamsho-Thomas
Odd as F*ck by Anne Walsh Donnelly
Muscle and Mouth by Louise Finnigan
Modern Medicine by Lucy Hurst
These Mothers of Gods by Rachel Bower
Sin Is Due To Open In A Room Above Kitty's by Morag Anderson
Fauna by David Hartley
How To Bring Him Back by Clare HM
Hassan's Zoo and A Village in Winter by Ruth Brandt
No One Has Any Intention of Building A Wall by Ruth Brandt
Snapshots of the Apocalypse by Katy Wimhurst
Demos Rising
Exposition Ladies by Helen Bowie
A Dedication to Drowning by Maeve McKenna

Social Media:

@fly_press (Twitter) @flyonthewallpress (Instagram)

@flyonthewallpress (Facebook)

www.flyonthewallpress.co.uk